Let's learn some interesting facts about Brazil!

Brazil

For Kids

People, Places and Cultures

Children Explore The World Books

SPEEDY
PUBLISHING

Speedy Publishing LLC
40 E. Main St. #1156
Newark, DE 19711
www.speedypublishing.com

Brazil is the largest country in South America.

The name Brazil comes from a tree named brazilwood.

Brazil is the only country in South America that speaks Portuguese.

Brazil is the 5th largest country in the world by both land area and population.

In Brazil they drive on the right-hand side of the road.

Brazil shares a border with all South American countries except for Chile and Ecuador.

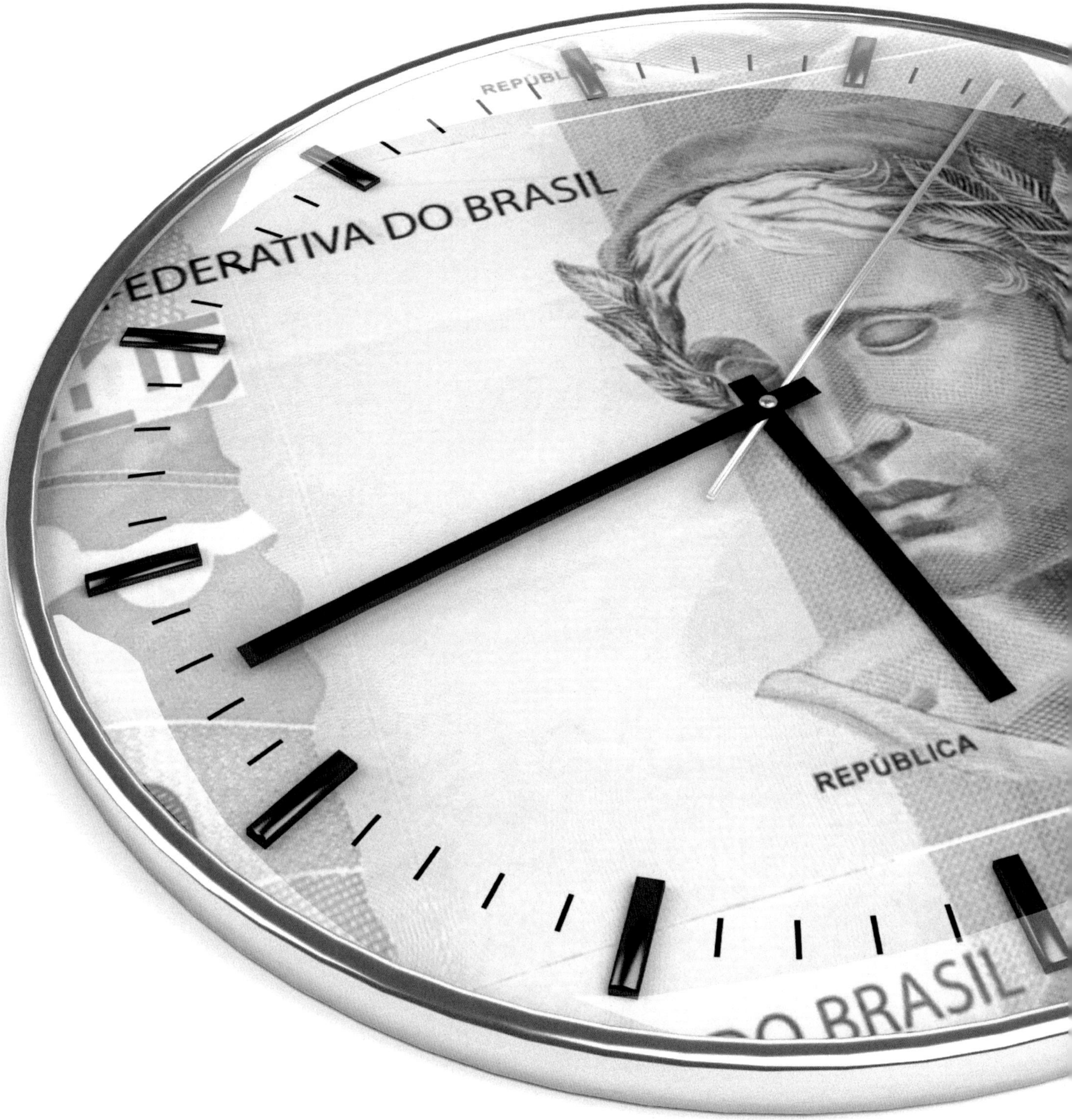
REPÚBLICA
FEDERATIVA DO BRASIL
REPÚBLICA
DO BRASIL

**Brazil covers 3
time zones.**

The Amazon River flows through Brazil, it is the 2nd longest river in the world (after the Nile).

Around 60%
of the Amazon
Rainforest
is located
in Brazil.

Iguazu Falls is an amazing waterfalls can be admired at the Brasilian border with Argentina.

The climate in
the majority of
Brazil is tropical.

Brazil is home to a wide range of animals, including armadillo, tapirs, jaguars and pumas.

There are around
2500 airports
in Brazil.

Football (soccer) is the most popular sport in Brazil with the national team consistently among the best in the world, winning the World Cup a record 5 times.

Over 5,000 people visit Brazil's most instantly recognisable landmark every day, Christ, the Redeemer, in the Tijuca Forest National Park.

Brazilians love their fresh fruits and vegetables such as okra, coconuts corn and beans.

The most favourite
dish in Brazil
is probably the
feijoada, a bean
stew made with
pork and rice.

Brazil has a lot to offer and you should visit the country soon and explore!

Made in United States
Orlando, FL
09 May 2023

32976811R00024